Nothing Wasted

A collection of spoken word pieces

Anthony Rivisto

DEDICATION

To my wife, Rebekah. You are my best friend, my love who dares to dream for the more that we were created for. You are my fearless love and I thank you for being my partner in this adventure. For the R.O.Y.A.L., my Jove!

And to my daughter, Amariah. You inspire me to dream and create! So, this is a first step of many, Daddy wants you to see your parents dream and pursue those dreams. Let them be a starting point for you, to reach higher and more often for God's best for your life.

TABLE OF CONTENTS

Dear Reader,

This is a compilation of the pieces I have written throughout my life. I use the word 'pieces' to represent each poem or spoken word written. They represent pieces of myself that I share like windows into my inner workings and how God invaded that place, bringing glory in the unexpected.

That is one of the reasons why I titled the book, Nothing Wasted. When we explore the deep areas in our lives - emotions, traumas, lies we believe or fears we struggle to face - it can seem hard to imagine the redeeming qualities. Yet, time and time again, I watched how God would take the ashes I handed Him, line by line, and create something that was beautiful and hopeful, where those qualities seemed foreign. His faithfulness has been constant in my life, so I present this book to give honor and glory, above all, to Him.

You may recognize that in each piece there is a certain level of tension. This is the other reason for this book as each piece represents a different aspect of yearning for the fullness or maturing of the seed that God has planted in me. My hope is that there will be pieces that inspire that tension inside you - to not settle for settling, but to wrestle with that greatness planted in you that is designed to be made manifest.

So, as you read this, feel free to jump around, find a piece that sticks out to you. Speaks to you. My writings that once were only for me are now yours as well. I hope they bring you encouragement, inspiration, and most of all, hope. That in the midst of whatever season, situation or setting you find yourself in... that you would know that God's love is capable and constant enough to take whatever you give Him, and shape it into something incredible.

"The beatings made blessings, in His hands there's reason that in all things, we were made to stand and... begin."

Thanks for reading,

Anthony

1. Fear

I don't want to share what I have,
because I fear,
I fear what may happen that hinders,
I fear reactions as tinder
of some fire of destruction,
I fear distractions
and the impending interruptions.

So, I proclaim this fear
like a loud percussion
declaring my immovability
though somehow
that never was
what was wanted...
To stand here...
To wait.
Intentions are irrelevant
in the face of opposition,
or really the figments that shadow
my imagination
I am "just in case" – ing...
Encasing any element of chasing,
because protection and comfort
become supreme and key to my embracing
when fear, is all that I'm evading...

Lost in the spiral of control,
avoiding the potential
for a known lesser
even though its stressors
are active oppressors
in my self-created society,
sipping its dwelling is a constant.

Time for sobriety...

And the taking of the R-I-S-K of sharing,
the leap of caring,
finding speech to spare for each
seed that may be daring
to sprout.
The soil cries out in the midst of decay,
hoping that life will spring forth and have its way,
while the fertilizer waits
in the breaking down of the old,
dormant in it's smelly abode...
What could possibly grow, here?

And yet we go there,
knowing circumstances don't point
to green lights,
but the red...
But the red...
as I have read
is significant in other means,
His blood covering,
making murky scenes
clean,
constantly using things
we think are one-sided,
reminded
of what is actually happening
as we hear.
The Voice that matters
silences the chatter...

there is only One
whom we
should fear.

2. Cliff Diver

I'm just not interested in pausing at the moment.

Feet leaving cliffs and the calling
is the ocean,

or motion in the waves that I aim at,
hoping...
are leading to pages, lessons,
making next seasons in my moments..

called to submission.

Fully independent or in-dependence
upon God's intuition,
given through faith in His Son.

All that I face in the midst of the sums life gives,
feeling detracted and divided,
while His passion only multiplies within the recession,
creating life,
denying the depression,

so I question if it has to remain.
For I know that His name
will call knees to lower frames,
provoking all to come face to face
with the reality,
so hidden in the midst of this race.

Still it is there,
and will be clear,
but we have only right now,
here...

So I stare out
gazing upon a sea of eyes,

I speak to them, to rize,
awake from your sighs
and find the edge
where you aren't willing to leap from.

That cliff...
                    is where I speak from.

Restrung are guitar strings broken,
because I was fearful to re-strum
what I had sabotaged in the face of rejection.
Pacing from the questions
that only led me back to that ledge
with good intentions,
but a lack of action to my pledges.

Soon, time passes

and the only feet nearing movement
is this feat of fear that's not moving
from this deep, dark pit of my stomach...
so I retreat... and my heart goes with it.

Many years have passed
and this place has lost its same
gasp-for-air feeling
of your breath being taken.

Now, when I visit,
it only seems to be a remnant
of what was,
or what could have been...

it's then that I wish I could go back!

awakening feet
to leap from cliffs
to find waves

to crash face first into!

"It's still in you..."

He speaks.
The Author
and needless to say
Finisher,
Who speaks best...
And He's right...
It never left.

But what did is my willingness
to let it which still exists
be free to be
what it was created for.

However,
my alternative
is to stay on the cliff
and watch it die before my eyes...

Don't settle for the view.

3. Standing

Lord, I come before You with my rags and my burdens.
A fragmented heart and consistent turning,
I'm yearning to make perfect
in all of my striving,
yet I know that You are purging
in the midst of my dying.
Providing
peace to this heart
that's adjusting to the healing.
Learning these new customs
of being loved and redeemed,
it's a wonderful thing...
that comes with a sting,
because when we come before You,
Your plan is to bring
it up and out,
erupting like shouts,
overcome with the feeling that Your love wins out,
and we, I,
stand here humbled by the process.
While somehow intimidated by the still
present nonsense
stating its lies and its fears,
denying every clear, promise, presence...
You persevere,
preserve me to be right now and right here...
So, here,
You have it!
All that I am to share.
Not prepared any more than my thoughts and my cares,
just me standing...

That's all,
standing...
no more.
Not special singing,

but more moans rising up from the core,
my aim is to pour
all that I am before You.
Recognizing my desire to resist,
as my tendency is to soar off
towards comfort
and known safety,
but You won't adjourn
until I reside in the heat of Your baking,
the meaning of Your breaking and molding,
shaping and consoling,
making me more by the weight of Your glory...

Wait... Lord, Your glory...
that rests on us like anchors to our walls,
changes to our halts,
reversing their direction as if gravity
was all focused on me,
stripping each thing that I
hope might keep me hidden,
like forbidden lies I still believe,
yet You receive my worship like burnt offerings
and respond to a yielded heart
with still, soft speech:

"Be free."

And truly,
tears can't be prevented from exiting,
carrying the pain and the bitterness
now battering down the breach,
it's time for release
and rest in His peace.

Standing.

4. Identity (Don't Envy)

In my life, I found an intersection
I had to stop chasing others' grace
And embrace my own reflection
And by faith see a face that knows his blessings
In my eyes, wise, despite the foes that press in

So I changed direction
and stayed attentive
to the King on the throne,
who honed me in my toughest testing
So I'm stressing,
to each and every brethren
Keep the faith
and don't allow the recollection
Or re-collecting
of past occasions or past depressions
Like second guessing,
you're pacing... facing the wrong direction
So that's where I'ma step in,
and begin inspection
Of the lies intertwined
in the sighs you're expressing

It's deception from the enemy
that makes you feel less than
When you give him your eyes,
you're behind his lines
Like an Iris behind fences.
I hear your cries, but they're met with
Second guessing
and an entertaining of the questions
That leave you losing
chasing confusing confessions
That don't leave the chest
they just cloak your lungs like vests
In this combat

where you keep the wrong camp
embedded in your vision,
so I'm headed on this mission
to be testing
What it is you're impressed with,
don't envy, because your identity, when you find it
Is this world's remedy... so let it be.

5. Rain

Welcome back rain,
welcome back storms.

I guess it has come to the day
where we should stay in doors,
for when it rains, it pours...

but me, I'm just going to find my way outside,
because I was made to face these storms.

You see, I rise up,
every time I see it strike.
Hoping that maybe,
it will pause all the storms in my life.

I guess it's how I escape, but
late at night I write to hear the whispers...
He's speaking.

So I offer up my fears
for the kneading of this heart,
for the purpose of deep seeding.
Planting blessing in the place of pain -
just what I've been needing.

I have seen courageous young people
reflect His love through the bleeding
and saw how He took dry bones
and recreated a being.

The beatings made blessings in His hands
there's reason that in all things
we are made to stand,
and begin.

By healing,

I dance in sequence.
Rain changes from falling to sprinkling
and His presence is all that matters to me.
This walk in our lifetime
is similar to breathing.
You've got to take in the truth
and exhale the pieces,
that scatter to the roof of your mouth,
just speak it out,
that stain of the pain,
for those eyes be seeking
to pull down your speaking.

For every word you utter
causes chains to be released
in this game for souls and speeches.

For out of man's mouth
come the heart's deep secrets
and the truth
is the devil's weakness.
So he preys upon you keeping
of your wounds and scars, his leeches -

sucking all life
from the children of the King,
it's time to rise again
for the time has come to see this
war for what it is,
find higher plains to preach this
message about the Truth,
all of you must believe this
war has already ended,
God's defeated all the legions.
Lighting the way for all His kingdom.
Letting His light shine through our lives
to those who need this.
For all can be redeemed

and brought back to freedom.

God is here,
that is what I'm teaching,
amidst the wandering and wondering
of what's the reason,
for the constant change in season
and the freezing of the frozen,
I'm speaking to you chosen.
To answer the call spoken over your lives.
Receive this love
so that you may open your eyes
and witness the precious thoughts He has for you,
more than the stars in the skies.

For you, He cries,
to the North, "Give them up!"
...and to the South, "Do not hold them back!"

For you are sons and daughters of the King,
my friends,
that is a fact.

6. Crowd Pleaser

Like Im'a clone quotes from pistols toted
so as to stretch that bullet they're evoking,
barrels smoking
smoldering it's contents,
emboldening a flavor
that I see you savor,
which tempts me...
to labor for my neighbor.
Impressing them like pens
leaving marks on paper,
only to linger for moments,
but away it's floating...
like vapors,
reminding me
that I can't live to be an entertainer,
because I'll be chasing after the wind
instead of chasing it's Maker.

I guess I grew up thinking
that I had control over the morale of the team
like a peacemaker.
This charge had me selling every piece
so I could keep it afloat,
not knowing my very gift
was being sold...
for scraps,
pawned off for temporary caps
over cemetery stones.
Now I see that this behavior
had been hereditarily honed,
like a clone replicating it's host,
there's something wrong with this picture,
I can feel it the most.

But I guess if you are good,
then I'm not supposed,

to show discontent...
It's rude and only breeds disruption
to the happiness we are all feeling.
So just fight that feeling,
and write us appealing rhymes
that rise the eyebrows
through reading and oh's the mouth is revealing,
that we yearn for something more.
Despite where we are
we know in our core
that we were meant to soar,
higher than before.
And higher is in store,
or rather stored within our pores,
it's ingrained in who we are
to be drawn.... closer.

Moving closer,
to the One
Who causes us to be moved,
Who pauses with us
when we lie consumed,
by this world's cares,
feeling compelled by dont's and do's,
He shows the truth,
that there is freedom,
not needing to compose,
only to cling to His words
because they bring life to those,
that hear them and do them.
I'm trusting, He's using,
all of my past and my living for approval
to realize that He is the only one that I need to please.
Peace... comes from laying down a burden
you were never intended to carry.
Redirecting your concern
to the purpose for which
you were birthed to be baring.

It's in this moment
that you've got to ignore the eyes on the side
glaring, staring, hoping to grab your attention,
asking for you to tarry and hesitate
from stepping into your mission.

Speak your heart, follow your passion,
let THAT lead your decision and ask yourself,
when the world is going one way,
and you know it is the wrong direction,
will you stand despite all who stand to question,
and be that voice... of dissension?

"Am I now trying to win the approval
of human beings, or of God?
Or am I trying to please people?
If I were still trying to please people,
I would not be a servant of Christ."

Galatians 1:10

7. Drink From The Well

(Your time with God is for you. Don't be so quick to share it with others, when He gave it to you to receive first. Drink from the well...)

Lord, breathe deep into my soul
fill every crack and crevice
so that I get it
and am to the full.
Let me pull on Your coattails
and desire more of Your grace for me
no longer passing it along
like a charitable throng...
I recognize that to be wrong
to give away what I was meant to receive;
to fill the place of hunger
with some need to feed others'.
Out of starvation, I proceed.

Lord, grant me the sweet manna
that is meant for me,
forming in me LIFE that comes ABUNDANTLY,
which cannot be contained or framed
like a presentation painted and hanged
to proclaim some moment of past time change
when God came down.
Lord, Your presence and Your speaking
is always... right now.
And more than enough to pour out
overflowing expectations
purging clouds to Son breaking
turning 'round the unmistaken
recognition of child meeting parent
fulfillment in the filling of voids
tears cried out meets embrace
and love is redefined, now
in this place where silence speaks

19

and hurts are healed.
Hearts revealed in the sanctuary of God (Psalm 73:17)
paused is the spending of time
suspended as perspectives perspire eternity
dripping on thirsty land...

surging,
waking
breaking.

Power collides in quakes and shaking,

but making new in this place
of rearranging,
renovation,
restoration
renewing...
transformation.

Seeking His reflection.

Drink from the well...

8. Unfinished (still fighting)

It's like knowing I have a deep, deep "potential" while
hating that word for its reminders of the yet to have
been realized hopes.

Seeming to only access this victory
through keycards gained
by placing a mask over the pains and
an act over the aches,
because if they were to ever show their face,
I would somehow be disqualified,
or a clock would run out on the time
that it takes to enter this race...
whole...
restored...
atoned and acknowledged.

You see,
I was born with an ability to "glean knowledge,"
like when I see you react in anger
I learn to be a changer,
avoiding your reactions by how
polished I can make myself.

Later,
built into a manipulator
in order to preserve my health.

Sad thing is
that the very "cure"
is a wealth of disease,
because it places my protection
in the hands of a thief,
learning to steal each piece
of security
by offering up my actions
as some form of surety,

knowing this is my only means
to ensure some peace.

So, I take these moments to slumber
instead of sleep...

Rest.... for my head piles stress
on shoulders now tense,
because I have run out of a means
to lie to my sense,
that there has been pain
and whether it was meant
or intended,
when I was raised,
there were hurts
where I learned
to pretend
and rearrange
my mentions
or redirect my sentence
aimed at re-framing
and prevention.

You hurt me
and somehow I learn
to cling to your protection,
"oh...that's, that's my bad!"
has been a common that I have allowed to exit,
until my mouth exhales,
boomeranging to ears
and I begin to believe
that I meant it...

and I let it,
settle in
like condensation rings
into wooden coffee tables,
impressions in chairs

after many nights
indented to bear
a new character...
it becomes a part of you.

Not the original intention,
but a wearing that speaks
to the decline now calling
through the seams un-mended...

Untended,
conversations un-ended,
because we never truly began to speak to what lies
dormant,
this need to be freed,
and now this need to speak,
so as to give speech
to the me that has been afraid to breach
walls erected to protect from the beast,
in any way that it would devour,
but it is alright now for me
to speak to those showered
by neglect, inability, doubt,
burdensome feelings that there is a cost
to work out,
a debt to be covered
for your life...
I don't know why I have allowed this until now,
but I do know that it drove me to find
true love without doubt
or debt,

because He took the parts of my life
that I felt had no place
and He calmly picked me up
and wiped off my face.
He covered me, protecting me
when I went my own way,

and He waited for the right time,
the right moment,
the right place..
still I didn't change,
He sent me people who could place
an answer to my hurts,
an acknowledgement of the pain,
He walked with me faithfully
and called me by name,
spoke to me as a Father
leading his son with true grace,
I owe it all to God who has brought me out and
makes a way...
so I'm writing,
exhaling the poison I would take,
that would hope for my decomposing,
corroding in the grave.
Instead I'm reciting poems...
placing power in its place
to bring the strength of a titan...
Be encouraged, as I am.

He is risen,
I'm unfinished,
but still fighting.

9. Growing Pains (Just A Thought)

Often times
We decipher our identity
by sifting out the pieces
and deleting all the enemies.
Seeking to be extended peace
while reaching to be settling
wrestling, leading to questions
I'm needing more than guessing,

stressing, been the mode of expression
since adolescence
or maybe just a means for permission
to be protected
seeing all that's missing
dismissing all of the blessings
equals a bitter perspective
in need of learning the lessons.

Testing came, when the world gave me blows
shattering my speech
He rewired my prose
desired to know if I'm "done yet?"
so, I chose to go
leaving what was lost
so i'm caught in a new role

Or a call,
disputed in the fall
deciding whether or not
I would choose to throw it all away,
that's when He taught me how to pray
to lean not on my own,
but alone upon His grace.

10. Deeper now...

Steadily settling into a session
that's severing all ties to distractions.
Speaking between these lines
and seeping deep into the captions.
Capturing the passion
that ignites in the basking
of His presence.

I'm asking for more,
of the One that I adore.
Pouring into the core what's been lacking,
evidence in the cracking of pores,
sores on the surface,
and this moment of searching
leads to the source of my burden,
hiding undisturbed because I rarely venture
beyond the shallow,
leaving my position to wallow
amongst the known stressors,
but He calls me not to be less than
anything I see,
but a reflection of His tenancy in me.
A reflection that transforms all that I see.
Blurred vision clearly renewed.
Removing all that was severely construed
due to a lack of nutrition.
Malnourished soul needing His hand and provision,
bridging all division
in the midst of my lack of decisions.
Grasping forgiveness in the faith of what You've done,
recharging batteries broken from
the bruises and battering
that happens when I choose to lean on
my own commander-ing of this ship.
Own wielding of this gift.
For my own uplift...

auto-pilot has flown without a direction
so I hand over the wheel
to He who planned the trip.
Finding peace in this dip
from my own heights.
Knowing You preserve and purpose my life.
Letting go in this dive,
high to the depths of the sound,
finding peace in this place,
deeper now.

"Where can I go from your Spirit?
Where can I flee from you presence?
If I go up to the heavens,
you are there;
if I make my bed in the depths,
you are there.
If I rise on the wings of the dawn,
if I settle on the far side of the sea,
even there your hand will guide me,
your right hand will hold me fast."

Psalm 139: 7-10

11. Night Run

Jogging the memory
like a path I've run before.
Where feet meet spots
ingrained with prior steps,
assuring that this evening's adventure
is launched from the platform
of invested time.

Ingested like air swallowed
to stretch lungs.
The dives get deeper and deeper,
enabling the eyes to adjust to the dim "scapes",
admiring the pearls laid here.

So we stay here
a little while,
until the wrestling learns resting
and the mind retires to the smile,
and nod,
because the spirit man
got the itinerary covered.
Silencing the smothering
of extra stimulation,
less being accomplished
while the more is evaded,
redundant statements,
but abundance is waiting
in the place that is hidden.
Not from but for,
invited to the table
to imbibe in the galore.
Or take time in the pure,
peaceful presence I adore.

Bringing a stillness to the water,
revealing the film that hovered

is now settling back down.
Settle down.
In this pasture that is vibrant and serene.
I am planted in Him
yet at liberty
because He is here.
We are here,
where grass blades sway
as branch leaves greets breeze
that maneuvers and orchestrates,
all in one gracious gift of ushering in the winds.
And the grin is in
this exhilarating place of rest and rejuvenate.
Blessed to recuperate
from stress tethered to ingested thoughts,
only caught as I take time to intertwine
His thoughts and mine,
like the needle's eye,
I relinquish my ties
to replenish my sights.

Washed and purged,
posturing first
to be brought to return
as my steps meet imprints
laid here before.

12. Go Outside

I like to take walks at night.
Inviting the cold to hold tight,
or at least lately that's how the night's been - cold.
Bringing a silence to the fold.
Honestly, that's when I feel right... in my mode,
inviting me to know a time when I don't
respect my surroundings.
Or rather don't neglect my Maker,
because I'm caught up in the bounding
of my environment;
distracted by the in's and out's of
what's next,
whose request
was left
in my inbox
for me to intox-
icate my need
to be high off interactions,
I'll be alright... after my "scratching"...
allowing for a revising of my actions
to shape my new need,
and how so subtly I steal attention
from He who designed me
to be free
from oppressing things,
but also free to become
an impact...

in this world that yearns to be startled,
shocked and awed
into a reason to be parted,
separated from the mundane,
invited to a changing of the inner makings,
leadings, bringing motivation to ensue breaking,
enduring the portraying of a happier day,
because they have now found truth

and they can't go on
fake...

So, I go back outside...

where the stars bring light
as the streetlights
act as lamps unto my feet,
igniting my sight as my thoughts seek
to know more,
to ponder this present time
where I know more is in store,
and yet is unrevealed,
sealed for an appointed time
or just sealed like presents unwrapped,
waiting on hands bold enough
to ask,
ready enough to stand
and receive...

I have resisted establishing
for moments when I feel it had a piece
of what I felt inside, but something told me...
to wait,
"great" forcing me outside again,
to run,
green lakes are dark at night
and the shadows hold challenges
to the sum inside of me,
but that some'n inside of me
is greater than he,
so I allow it to steadily
ready my cadence,
knowing that my trust in Him
builds patience, boldness
in the statements,
and His hope is made great
as I empty my trust in me

and place it in hands
that hold and part seas,
inside,
the waves find peace.

The end of my night
brings a wakening of more need
for the Spirit in me.
While it shares a promise
to clearly speak
and for me that means
in the midst of my nights.

So, when its late,
and I take the time,
I force myself
to rise,
and go
outside.

13. This Hope

I sit at this keyboard
like its Murder She Wrote,
shaking off the slumber
that I almost let soak
me into a nap,
taking me back to dream-filled scenes
with blurry lines like trees.
"They look like men,"
but am not sure of the sight I see.
It's fighting me, inside
like an ache that knocks deep,
I struggle with the inkling
that there is way more in me
than I am living out,
giving out,
spilling out of my willingness
to be transparently in doubt,
while being allegiant to His grace...
working out with fear
and trembling, this faith
that does not exist exempt
of change,
in our hearts, in our minds,
life and death cannot share the same space,
yet I feel this tension.

Like dissension and division
contained in a dialogue to decide
the recipients of the decision-
which way will you go?
Whose way will you follow?
Because there is a narrow strait to truth
and there is a wide path of sorrow.
Different means
with different ends indeed,
and this tension that you see

working out inside of me
isn't just an outward expression,
it is an inner well rising up
awaiting its procession,
unmet with resistance,
for it seems that when it comes down to this mission,
the opposition lacks jurisdiction
but what it is given...

Yet, it is given...
the bars,
the chains,
the stalls,
the crimson
stains like paint that line the walls of our prisons,
not knowing we face monsters
that our actions have risen
from small, minute
pursuits of passion
in instants,
sinking back in abysmal
imaginative revisions,
that if this would just happen
then it would all for once click,
then click,
time's spent
and you get
just this,
opportunity to realize that this cycle
won't switch
in the might
that you're born with,
it's hopeless,
but know this...

there's hope.

And now Lord,

what do I wait for?
My hope is in You.
Deliver me from all my transgressions

This hope I am confessing
is that in the midst of my lowest moments,
Jesus invites me to blessing,
incites me to correction
for freedom from depressing
burdens, that are heavy
and yokes that cause turning,
from the original intention.
There is hope
and living it out,
because the work is done
and has ended.

So I have hope,
because I accept it.

* Psalm 39: 7-8

14. Inspiration

deception'll get ya

if you let it
it'll set you up
for a lecture
that recites legislature
to hold you down from grandeur.
They fear Commander
so they fight the stander
challenging the standard
and hoping you'll stay clear
sowing you to wait there
and grow cold in the damp air
moldy and despair
they boast in depression
that just like them
it'll leave you too...
guessing...
stressing...
only to accept it...
you are less than....

So the darkness claims like it's got ya,
and the prosecutor sits from accosting.

"Any last words?"
they invite you to bid in...
or better yet,
give in...

Feeling the chains they've laid on you
with every word
leaves you set
like stains
in a grimace that begs
for rest,

but deep inside
behind the lies,
lies a tiny spark of light
that reminds you to
take a step...
and so you do,
rising from the chair,
back bent,
leaning to the left,
you take all strength
and wince with each breath
to lift limbs and chains
and frame broken, but left..
to your direction
and you lead to another step
and another
leading to the bench,
and slowly approaching
you notice your light has been growing
only to see inside your chest..
as it starts... to glowing,
inside knowing
there is release awaiting,
like tears meeting air,
so you make feet meet the pavement
of the foundation cracking
as you make your way to the center,
all eyes glare as they prepare
to enter
into devouring,
anticipating cowering under pressure,
chains dangle at the center...

and you pray.

Lord, I know that You made me,
created me to break free,
and if ever You would save me,

I pray that You would make these,
chains shatter at every clasp,
and restore me to my proper stance....

and as if a whisper caught my glance,
I am told...

"be free."

So ... like Autobots and Bumblebee,
a rumbling happens inside of me,
reigniting a flame that was hiding
to keep from sputtering,
now spreading, inside...
flames flutter through veins
to meet pores
to flex joints
inviting every muscle to awake,
multiplying my pace,
I am amped by the gauge of the Spirit,
electrifying the space....
illuminating each face,
burnt away is
disgrace, depression, mistakes,
what lessened their ways
to settle for a stake
in a world that won't wait
for their hope to be made real,
it is all burnt away
as the refusal to give in is revealed,
no longer concealed
is the light that lies inside
awaiting to meet this fight...

so I rise in the midst of the people....
in the midst of this room
where once my enemies were awaiting
my succumbing to the evil

of what is called reality...
however, what was real for me
has been changed by Who I allowed in me.

So I look around... and breathe.
And see that it is no longer me
all the eyes are engaging,
but a presence in the room
that is now re-engaging,
bringing each heart to face up,
like a standing ovation,
and reclaiming what was lost is now found,
amazing.

My inspiration.

15. Let Me Have My Way

As I sit here, I realize I have nothing left to say.

My words are dried up
like a spigot tapped out,
it is time to find my source.
So, pray...
Which brings me to think.
About the many things I do
to appear to be following
the God I serve,
but I fear it to be hollow,
so I swallow in smoke to reflect this present time.
Not necessarily a bad place I'm in,
but greatness haunts me like a long-lost friend
who I try to recall once again,
yet am only left with a reminder that old greatness
has come and went
and here I am.

Or rather, here I sit.
Recognizing, that this friend still
calls me from the deep,
places I know,
but forgot how to keep
conversation afloat,
because the standard's too steep
for me to carry when I flow
in this shallow stream.
Hoping that deep
will somehow be instilled in me,
despite my resistance to the abyss
of what I don't know to be.

"I know what He has for me"
is a statement I've allowed to limit my destiny.
So I'm questioning,

the place where I am
and whether I clearly see.

Despite me, He is still revealing,
returning me to knowledge of a feeling,
a presence of peace,
that only is and can only...
be.
Instincts...
explanation fails
so still I strive to speak,
out what is inside
confiding that I know He breathes,
life into my lungs
despite the air I breathe.

So I seek,
desiring to know that cold...
I embrace it with flushed cheeks,
soaking in the light that I gain
when I spend time silencing,
all the good habits and plans I preach,
to myself
hoping that my plan might be,
good enough to attain true freedom and peace,
without having to offer up my heart
and go through surgery.
A reluctant speech,
I reluctantly receive,
knowing that the Voice I have heard
has called me to the deep...
For that is where this Voice comes from,
echoed in the strums of the wind
and within I am met by numbs
of cold that hold my flesh, to inset a stun
settled to challenge my spirit to spite the cold
and come to find out what is on the other side.

I have a choice
that only lies on the other side...
and the key is in me,
in my fear..
and in my pride.
They are the prices I must pay
to answer this invite
that I hear in whispers
like whiskers leading the blind.
So I write,
a last letter to myself,
reminding me to fight...
"You either live like a coward
or stand up and die,
to who you think you are
and what you have figured for your life,
are thoughts that will never amount
to His promise to provide.
So stop the strides
that you know are in vain and
return to the last place
you know that you heard Him say,
roll the dice
and let the chips fall where they may...

I have a plan for you, so let Me have My way.

16. The Process

I close my eyes tonight in anticipation.
Knowing the journey I've been taking
is one led by the One and His placing
of adventures and obstacles.
He mentors my "possibles"
through intentional pauses full
of listening and hearing,
do you hear me?
Ingesting what is taken in
to break down the nutrients –
new sequences and frequencies;
relenting from decency
to reverence coming from frequently
standing on tippy toes.
Reminding the,
presence we,
neglect to recognize.

(Selah)

In His image,
it's in our eyes,
but living like it's in disguise,
this inner fight to be revealed,
when this tension only exists for us
to learn to yield,
to His grace...
unearned favor shaking our faith
to be wrecked and changed.
Our "yes" became
a resting place
for the seed to grow,
and as the ground breaks
and makes its way,
we see the slow,
abrupt,

overwhelming display
of His love
– in and through.

Beginning a new
perspective of how we see this undertaking,
faith being made into faith,
we embrace the Sovereign
and He displaces our bottling,
uncorked to pour out,
posturing to use spouts
installed at our weaving,
activated by our believing,
rivers of living water flowing like streams,
into the sediment,
causing life to spring from barren wastelands
and paths to be made in the wilderness,
His precedent.

His will is this,
that none should perish,
inviting us all to the beautiful sanctuary
of repentance,
in His presence
are complete joy and pleasures,
restoring to full measure.
Settling the stirring and concerning
to rest into His endeavors,
desiring for another excuse
to ren-dez-vous,
I mean rendezvous,
parlez vous?,
His language comes from
listening and exchanging,
and it's changing, me,
as I take His speech
and relate statements that
exhale from the pauses,

I am learning
and practicing
to trust
(and enjoy)
the process.

"If anyone thirsts,
let him come to Me and drink.
He who believes in Me,
as the Scripture has said,
out of his heart will flow rivers
of living water." - John 7:37-38

"Behold, I do a new thing,
now it shall spring forth;
shall you not know it?
I will even make a road
in the wilderness
and rivers
in the desert." - Isaiah 43:19

"The Lord is not slow
in keeping his promise,
as some understand slowness.
Instead he is patient with you,
not wanting anyone to perish,
but everyone to come to repentance." - 2 Peter 3:9

"You make known to me
the path of life;
you will fill me with joy
in your presence,
with eternal pleasures
at your right hand." - Psalm 16:11

17. The Mind's Prison

I will arrive at the level to which I strive.
My stumbling blocks aim to deprive
me from seeing more than one side of myself
or rather even the whole.
As obstacles aim to create holes and voids,
I can hear the noise,
but they are not worthy of invoking choking
upon my soul;
strangling my peace.
You see, my life will cease,
when my Creator decides.
Until then,
I'm gonna' increase the strength and dedication
and decrease the sighs.
I see these skies,
they watch me and they send me signs,
all that I translate through these lines
so as to lift weight off of my spine and neck bone.
Forged with the power to set in stone
and engrave my tone
or rather He who made me.
I've been struggling to find that path again lately,
waiting for the call,
falling to a season,
Fall brings Winter,
Winter brings freezing.

Still recollecting all the faceless beaten,
on their knees pleading,
not comfortable with the bleeding,
"What's the reason?"
is the aim of their meaning,
finding resting in the blessing
of their dreaming
and visions given,
all an answer to why we're living,

in destinations facing the purpose of our mission,
found through what we find is missing
in these stacked coins -
wells of wishing.

You see,
you're poor in life,
but you're rich in the world,
proud to be a man,
but you're dissing that girl,
seeing things as straight
when you know it's all a curl
in this circle of time.
Seeing Red, White and Blue,
when you know it's really just Purple at times,
letting people know what's really worth in their minds
and we question why we don't see
the birth of the crimes,
below the surface of signs,
find the truth in the lies.
Double deciding the repeating
of the words I choose to rhyme,
it's all a dime
within a ten-digit design
aimed to ask why we don't get the divine
when in vain we call upon it.
Due to our desire to cry when our body
doesn't get what is wanted,
possessed slaves carry the masks of the haunted
and are chased by demons among them,
but don't question why they're here,
question why we're running.

It's stunning
to realize your power.
I guess we're just hypnotized
by the passing of hours.
A generation called cowards,

fatherless and sour,
but the truth is ours.
The meek truly tower
with our voice behind the muzzle,
stolen piece to this puzzle,
dismissed rebuttal,
but the revolution is never subtle
and will always grow within the humble,
hunted, and chased,
within this system is not our place,
keep moving south.
With the faster rules to deploy the faster routes,
the mask of fools who decoy disaster's scouts
are among us,
but the wise are already told what it is all about.
So that one day,
our Master's tools
will destroy this master's house -
our time's mission.
But if you follow fools,
you will never make it out,
of your **mind's prison**.

18. Lies

Embedded deep inside
are memories that remind
me to live subject to a time
when I believed I wasn't His pride and joy.

Anything speaking contrary to His voice...
is noise.
Arrows and missiles deployed
to decoy Saints from fulfilling His mission -
to be salt and light
in the midst of darkness.
Proclaiming freedom to these prisons
where we find ourselves living.

Can you hear my spitting?

My speaking,
intended to highlight the meaning
that was meant when it was said that

      "It is for freedom, that Christ set us free."

So don't be deceived by lies that speak
against what He has already done.
We've already won,
but somehow I still lie caught in the sum
of what's been done
to and through me.
Still rehearsing the past
even though I passed it
the last time I asked Him
for it to leave,
while subtly I give permission
for the lies to be retrieved,
because deep inside
there is still a wound,

inviting like a room
where I allow it to move back in
speaking its doom.

We choose
to listen,
because it's easier to blame something else
instead of face it and forgive it
or better yet learn to accept forgiveness
of ourselves,
turning to face what lies
on the shelf,

hiding like stealth lies fly undetected,
but as long as they lie inside,
we remain unprotected.

Deception.

19. It Is Well

What is this interruption?

This chasm that exists like a spasm,
of muscles designed to run free,
extending and soaring on heights
only He can invite,
in spite of the present and near fear.
Doubt, He reminds us,
to break through.
Clouds that crowd around our eyes
to see skies
beyond
what lies...

Jesus, come in this place.

Enter in and change the atmosphere
where You alone are feared.
Peering through to see
Your throne,
holding You seated,
ruling and reigning
imbuing a prevailing wailing
to overcome the aching.

Jesus, our groaning exists,

because we are changing.
Making room for Your Spirit.
Come consume and infuse
our imagination to behold
Your majestic
that shatters fabrications
and restores what is cluttered.
Establishing revelation
of a new thing.

Here,
in the midst of the old.
10:10 told to those.
Inviting us to that deeper,
still water,
so I stop and pause
bearing witness as You hover.
Carrying provision
and prophetic vision
to see You in the midst of the storm.
To be soothed
as the missiles aim to bring hell...

It Is Well.

20. On The Ladder

Lord, sober my mind to see You clear,
when the enemy's lies tell me You're not near,
help me here.
Give me understanding in the midst of the storm,
blow in and transform
when my thoughts are clouded
by doubt and despair.
Worry taking over making me feel impaired,
not knowing You're there.
Whispering.
To know Thy strength, in weak moments,

[listen]

where You use it and hold it.
Molding me like clay
to peel away
the layers of false protection.
Defense mechanisms I've neglected
to face with intention,
only feeling their tension.
This all is worth the mention,
because in permitting another dimension,
subtracting by adding to -
it left division.
That never existed,
but persisted in the striving.
Fear taking hold.
Jesus, reshape me to hold Your glory.
Overflowing and succumbing to Your story.
I collide with You like a divine set up -
my weights and yokes meeting
Your breaking and revoking
of all my opposition.
Mind renewed
leaving my pursuit only of You

and not on evading the devil's wishes...
and in the midst it
provides me trust, and a release,
relinquishing my gripping...

So in my sitting,
my feet recognize the collection of dripping
water on these steps I have climbed
to perch upon,
I sigh and recognize all slipping
is now submitting
to Your peace
that stills the deep
with endless increase,
and lies...
they cease
as the Truth is known.

Taking upon my own
something that is gifted freely.
Inside I receive
and outside perceive
the changes that occur, when we believe.
Now displayed on the surface...
So let there be LIGHT,
to stand in the certainty of purpose
woven deep in the beginning,
And He's grinning
as you wake to the brimming
of His overflow,
poured out like laughter :)
finding pasture,
here,
on the ladder.

VISTO.

And David was greatly distressed;

for the people spake of stoning him,
because the soul of all the people was grieved,
every man for his sons and for his daughters:
but David encouraged himself in the Lord his God.
1 Samuel 30:6

21. The Box

If I know the way,
then your word is irrelevant-
obstacles keeping me from accomplishing my
settlement,
or present tense intentions
met with past tense perspectives
that keep you from seeing reality
or simply just accepting it...

Silly... how I can get so caught in this predicament.
I thought I was in the right
when it all seemed legitimate,
but slowly you faded from site...
and despite my efficient sense,
I found myself locked in the box,
unable to rescind the sent,
messages proclaiming points,
shooting arrows from this regiment,
aimed to imply the obvious
that you need to just accept and bless,
the plans I lay out
in the way I have rendered best.

Yes,

best,

I said it.

Can you see my pride in this?
I seem to hide from its rising
when I deny the voice inside...
maybe you need to just ride with this...
I say,
not recognizing your sighs in the midst,
I seem to only deny it

because I'm tired of this,
exchange,
I just need to explain
how it will happen,
slowly I choose to silence another,
allowing another thing's enacting.

Self-deception...
is the core of this lesson.

You think you are acting in the right
unknowingly making it wrong
as people, get neglected.
When person becomes opponent,
winners become irrelevant.

Living, breathing objects...

this is not an embellishment.
Needing more than intelligence,
but a reverence acquired
by perceiving another person...
instead of the upset to my temperament.
Unmet is the expectance
that we have to prevent this,
apathy of another
for our agenda's acceptance.
Unconcerned with the subtleties
if the accomplishment is pervasive,
and lacking the waves necessary
to cause any changes,
the box remains intact
while relationships strain.
How is it that it is so easy to misplace
value solely on ourselves
while others we forsake?
I can line this whole piece
with eloquently placed,

phrases
in the right cadence,
but if I don't consider you
in the midst of these statements,
theoretically I'm wasting
the purpose for creating...
To step outside that box
we find ourselves in,
and remember ways
that we wish we might live.
Despite this
it still happens a lot.
Now you just can't say
you didn't know,
about the box.

22. Intercession

Lord,
grant me a burden
to pull for Your service.
Into this fire burning away
and purging,
Your furnace,
where no infirmity can preserve.
Entering in by Your blood
we are purchased.
So, no longer can we lay on lay-away
hoping the next payment will serve us,
freedom through our pleading
and bruised knees yearning,
but finished,
sin is diminished
with closed and drawn curtains.
Our old has passed away
and our partnering
with Your strategies
bring about a preserving,
where light confuses darkness
and it has not overturned it.

So, teach me this confession.
That You,
the Interceder
bring us into all intercession.
Using us like Your fingers,
leading Your body in its direction.
I suppose that my only request
is to remind me of Your reflection.
That I may always live into Your intentions,
by trusting amidst the tension
and pushing against the selfish
tendencies in me
that only disconnect me

from Your presence.
I want to live life invented
by Your delights met in
my imagination,
many times I want it now
and can't wait for the patience,
yet my weakness only makes way
for Your strength to find a way (weigh -) in.

Jesus lead me
into all obedience
as Your call beckons further steps.
Yearning to be learning
more lessons with each breath.
Being stretched like lungs do vests
unable to prevent or contain,
it is breached and remains.
Your will, call, purpose, plan,
of which I humbly am all at Your service,
hands stretched out,
palms raised,
ready for Your perspective.
Lead me,
and us all,
into Your intercession.

23. Therefore

Because of
due to the fact that
based on this reality
you are
this is...
act accordingly.

I look at the many "therefore" occurrences
in and out of my life
that floated like clouds
lower than the altitude natural
to fog my vision.
Spoken like incisions,
intravenously clogging decisions,
diluting intentions
subtly serving others'
and solely surviving to be
"mentions",
suggestions
rather than statements,
like indented parts of a book
that stand out...
Washed out
were parts of my existence,
because I lived according to
therefore statements
that subdued my walk
and silenced my living.

Yet,
there is this reason.
That still is, breathing...
In every story
where life hasn't been all
that was **potential**.
Despite its lack,

it's back,
like a recurring plan of attack,
it will have its way in our life,
because the very meaning of life
requires this essential.

"Therefore
you are no longer a slave,
but a son,
and if a son,
then an heir of God
through Christ."

I look to define
what it means to be a son.
Called and loved.
Adopted in
and one who is accepted.
Admitted,
permitted and with intention.
You have been brought from out of
to within the family.
Therefore
you are:
accepted,
covered,
protected
and promised.

In place of the broken versions
of each of these spoken notions,
the reality of the truth
seems to sow them in moments
where you are proven
and provoked to decide
upon the "so what" of this therefore...

To either return to the clouds

of doubt
and denial of such love,
or acceptance
of this kindness
leading to repentance
from what once was
to now is.
The essence of transformation,
being sought out
because we are heirs
with a call and plan,
hand crafted,
carefully shaped in His hands,
therefore we can
live accordingly,
with faith found through digging down,
to know what He told us when we first found
home on the rock,
His love.
Therefore...

24. A Conversation

I suppose I exist to speak to the spirit.

To inspire the desire to shatter what we're fearing.
So I peer in through the window of the soul
and scream for the filling of light to the full.
It seems, to the naked eye, "why?" is the question.
Sitting from the lack of foundation
their resting seems stressing at best
and I sigh as I only aim to pry open the chest
meant solely to find treasure -
buried deep within weathered
pains that mark stretches,
cracks and crevices,
lying embedded in a stubborn direction,
yet never past protection
they find themselves still...
arrested in depression,
aching from the pressing
they either die or press in
to the Spirit that answers all questions
from stirring and sober minds alike.
I suppose it's just right now,
time to listen.

Time to listen.
Past the possible, probable, and the pension
sent in the mail for the pausing in procession.
No it's time for the passionate potency
that only comes from His presence,
yes... His presence
that shatters what we call presents
and reminds our mind to submit to God's destine
letting go we relinquish
our side of the story
He could have already read and written.

No surprise I hold the pen tripping,
sweat dripping
like His blood that already covered the sins missing,
yet I still struggle to find,
recollecting,
only RE-Collecting what's not there,
future regretting got me impaired like a blank stare
and the cycle sits there,
begging for a host,
debating every hope
'till the days are just coped in the gaze
like wave tattered boats and the tide comes in...
and it goes.
So I know,
more than ever,
that now is important,
as we sit here sorting out our falling short,
we need to just let go
and let God be our portion,
because the world is in need much more than you or I
could plead our case.

I suppose in our hands times wasted,
un-hasted
like it was all a dream
and our lives are encased in scenes
that can be reset and re-screened.

I'm lost in the thought that it is all a dream
aimed to steal vision from our eyes
and wisdom from the divine
replaced with missions to demise
through wishing for a fight
to remind us we are still living,
listen as these words exit my mouth
like arrows to your spine,
I want you to resign
from the thought that this spiral goes down

for often times the bottom
is when Christ is found,
and your light resounds,
despite the dark night and the hounds
that chased you around
not knowing it was only leading you
to right here and right now...

So, I write now,
to speak to your spirit,
arise in faith to spite what you're fearing,
for in the path I see a clearing
and your Creator is near,
in your pain and in your tears,
it's real, God LOVES YOU
regardless of what you've done
or how you feel.
So, like you are faced with a life or death situation
and the inside of your soul is aching
from silence stealing your statements...
It's either now or nathan.
Who's nathan?
nathan is nothing, named for something,
because you've become familiar with it's legacy of
shame
instead of forbidding it's limiting of your faith.

It's time to peer past the pain
and scarred hurts
and realize that change lies harbored
in the things unseen,
unseen like the offerings
given up in hopes of being brought past your tears,
yet those tears conquer fears
for the prayer of a broken and contrite spirit
pierce through this world's treasures like spears,
and life resets to clear what has been blurred.

And what has occurred
has been a conversation,
exhaling these statements
like inhalants to patients
knowing this quotient that cloaks the cold like blankets
and puts hope in old places.

Amazing grace upon grace concerning your situation,

have patience...

25. One Sitting

I'm convinced
that every time I take a moment to scribe my thoughts,
potential is tugged on
like that dog that's been waiting
for you to take him out for that walk,
and found in this talk
are dormant thoughts
not stopping at, but more than
just emotion,
meaning for the motions,
steaming from the potent
power of our day's encounters
aimed to grind us down
to a burnout bow
or something of the kind
that isn't much kind,
yet thus is life
and even more thus are the pieces
we are given;
however,
missing is our appraisal
of the ability to act in agility
responding with resiliency
often found in the humility
of the deep wells we call our souls.

As a Christian,
I still forget
that these deep waters
are more than I can stand in –
half way in and half way out
"catching my breath,"
hoping it will help in my depths
when I finally embrace them –
but there is a reason that it states that the deep
cries out to the deep in He,

knowing that in my living beneath,
I can rest in His ability
to help me breathe
and be my means
to accomplish all,
that now,
is His working.

One sitting,
and it sits in me,
a reminder to allow Him to work in me...
not a striving or justifying,
just defying the disguising
that I am accustom to trying,
His hands won't pry,
but point at sighs
that I exhale because I am sore
from the time spent at a pointless position....
And each moment, He prompts me
to begin, in Him,
a resting and allowing His pressing
to move through impressions
left in my chest to present
His presence through thoughts in each sentence
meant to cause a collection
of thinking in the listener
who reads them and
perceives a relation to what's clicking
and clinking
in them...
seeking to send
one more person
on a one-sitting session
to write what is pressing
deep in the tension
they are feeling.
One Sitting.

26. Go The Limit

I speed...
Weave through the traffic,
whatever I need to do
to be there the fastest,
caught up in the chase
I might, see you in passing,
but my eyes stay set on the preview of smashing,
moving, soundtrack inducing
a shift to gears that allow for the "vrooming",
or doing whatever I got to do
to beat you there,
when I'm in my truck,
I'm impaired
by this need to "get there"
and everything else is along for the ride,
seeming like when the morning comes,
I'm caught in stride,
one foot out the door
before the other can find,
a sock and shoe,
preparing to step right,
into the thick of the day...
So I end up speeding along my way...

With an accent like a dismay
my tempo lies changed
by this need to speed.
Knowing there are limitations I face
but taking that risk
I build habits that breach, the rules,
bend them for some reasons,
knowing that inside it's just my seizing
of another chance to jump the gun,
rather than build up patience,
steadily in a run
when I arrive I'll just be waiting,

what is it in the commute
that has me chasing? . . .

In the midst,
I hear God saying

"go the limit
...follow within knowing that it's Me up in it,
not yourself that's winning
in this racing your minds been chasing
rather than moving it's got you tasting
the truth but its root your disputing
with your actions,
slaving to your satisfaction
replace that with passion
and amazed you'll be basking at the pace
you'll relax in it patiently.
Just wait and see,
I know what I'm talking bout,
it's slavery when you're in this
running round,
and round it goes
until the spiral flows
back to the ground floor.
Welcome to acceptance.
This is where you grow.
Accept it.
No exceptions.
I won't leave you to be less than
who I meant for you to be,
so T, be bold and don't fold
to this world's motions,
I made you more than your emotions."

And I know that there will come a time
when I will need to find speed
to excel me on my way,
until then, I'll wait,

and let Him
set the pace.

VISTO

27. Strong Tower

I guess I confess
that I've let stress
press upon my chest
feeling stretched beyond regress,
but beyond regrets
be the pauses when
He uses all the STUFF
for His accomplishments.
Or presents
using the present
to present to them,
an encouragement
serving courage for discouraged men,
ensuring them
that He is surely purging all concerning
His servants in this mission
that isn't ever a mimic of gimmicks,
but a limerick to penetrate
the penitent hearts,
so I'm prostrate before the King
whose remarks re-spark the weak heart
and make it strong,
colliding with the violent
and rewriting their songs,
I'm residing in the private
where His whispers are psalms
that minister calms
even storms can't wake,
so I contemplate in this space
where I seek more than just His grace,
but His face.

Where I'm close enough
to feel the whiskers.
Quiet enough to hear the whispers,
invited in, delivered,

I confide in the Giver,
relying on His ability to be my lifter,
the Forgiver, who sees me clean,
washed free from every stain,
brought forth to begin again.
So I can stand, where I used to crumble,
humbled as I see each brick
bundled in an assembly
stones, in an ensemble medley,
setting as the mortar dries smooth.
I am brought to know
from the depths of my soul
that He uses each piece,
every inch and crease
that I would see as a blemish,
now somehow changed in this hour,
as I rest, secure,
in Him,
Strong Tower.

28. Intersection (2002)

What makes me think I know who I am?
I went back in time a couple a days ago
and I guess I forgot where I stand.
Or I went back in age,
my mind was cluttered by things such as
anger, bitterness, and rage.
I've been ready
to turn the page
and on to the next chapter.
Yet I find myself rereading my past
and not what comes after.

When does change happen..?
When you take the upper hand?
A look from above to see where you stand?
I looked from above and saw myself slippin'
Trying to find an excuse to why I am still trippin'.
Sittin' here reading my thoughts on where I am headed
to.
Like if my friend fights for me then I have to fight for
you.
But fight who?
That fist that hits could have hurt you
Or you, or you... or me.
2 years ago, I laid in a hospital bed
eating from an IV
Not a fatality, but it seems no different.

I'm standing on the sidewalk with a broken bottle
in my hand yelling out and
ready to take a stand.
But what am I standing for and who am I standing
against? I'm ready to hurt someone, but 10 minutes
later
it doesn't make sense.
Caught in the heat of the moment acting with no sense.

I hop in my car
driven back to my rest
focusing on a way to get my head straight
and relieve this stress.

Look up! Red Light. Stop! Intersection.

29. Awake

Alert, to His leading.
I'm typing to bring lightning
to the landscape of my slightly sensitive
heightened residence,
inviting His precedence to arrive in presence...
presenting open hands
with words like pillows
to rest Your ears,
smoke stirred up through fragrant tears,
I am here,
like fear

...where it should only be placed.
hungry, pursuing,
trusting, in faith.
Your presence comes
like a warm, fragrant rain.
Aromatically activating
all that inhabits this space,
enacting like grace
- this is undeserved.

Unrehearsed,
nor reserved,
but honestly undone.
Pausing to shun counterfeit sums;
religious puns
with hopes to latch on to speech propelled,
but the leaking of this compelling
is telling of projectiles that can't be contained.
Exhaling breaths from strained frames
that have bent to proclaim
through pains but remained,
through.
So, I remain...
in face of the Purger,

Who breathes upon my frame,
inviting a merger...
My Preserver,
who brings life to me,
and speaks right where I deplete,
to rewrite what I delete
and recites speech that only He can speak.
He's filling my exhaling,
instilling with each infilling
the voids I lift up
like holes in my soul,
that can no longer evade Him...

This is worship,
of the King who is higher.
So I bring my desire,
like sparks on kindling...
I breathe,
specifically to serve up a fire.
He in I,
rising up for my Sire,
pulled from the mire,
now planted on the rock,
dug down from the place
where He granted that I stop,
serving my affliction.
Circling, rehearsing what's missing,
in Him, it's dismissed in
the midst of forgiveness,
bore in the sins He took
and now I witness
like a recalling of events
carrying the weight of His imprint.

Humbled by the loss of what I deserve
and the gaining of what I do not.
Grace came fully for a sinner
that was caught,

unable to soar free,
now I spring forth like seeds,
in this journey that He leads
in each moment of abiding,
residing in this gliding of His winds,
and yet brought within His wings.

So I sing a redeemed anthem
that echoes His heart beat,
like speech given to that hidden
in plain sight,
that more might awake,
and take flight.

VISTO

ABOUT THE AUTHOR

Anthony Rivisto is a native Seattleite. His first love was basketball, followed shortly by writing, which found its way into his life through many nights spent "freestyling" with friends. His relationship with God is a major influence to his spoken word and has been a bridge of engaging God through the pieces that have come from writing from the heart.

Anthony hopes to inspire all who encounter his poetry to walk out the fullness of God's plan for their life and to know that in God's hands, there is Nothing Wasted.

Anthony is an Associate Pastor at Seattle Revival Center in Newcastle, WA. He and his wife, Rebekah Rivisto, and daughter, Amariah Rivisto, live in Renton, WA.

Victorious In Struggles To Overcome.

VISTO.